ESTHER'S GRAND
ADVENTURE

WRITTEN BY
Alyssa Johnston

ILLUSTRATED BY
Mercedes Showers

NEW YORK

NASHVILLE • MELBOURNE • VANCOUVER

Esther's Grand Adventure

Published in New York, New York, by Morgan James Publishing. Morgan James is a trademark of Morgan James, LLC. www.MorganJamesPublishing.com

The Morgan James Speakers Group can bring authors to your live event. For more information or to book an event visit The Morgan James Speakers Group at www.TheMorganJamesSpeakersGroup.com.

ISBN 9781683503163 paperback
ISBN 9781683503187 eBook
Library of Congress Control Number: 2016917632

Cover and Interior Design by:
Chris Treccani
www.3dogdesign.net

In an effort to support local communities, raise awareness and funds, Morgan James Publishing donates a percentage of all book sales for the life of each book to Habitat for Humanity Peninsula and Greater Williamsburg.

Get involved today! Visit www.MorganJamesBuilds.com.

Esther's Grand Adventure

This is Esther. Esther was an ordinary girl who dreamed of going on a grand adventure.

She lived in a teeny-tiny, old house with
her cousin Mordecai.

Mordecai had an important job, he was a gatekeeper at the King's palace. Which meant he got to see everyone who came to meet the King.

One day, Esther sat in her bedroom looking out her window.
She was thinking about what she wanted to be when she grew
up and picturing all the adventures she would go on.

Just then, Mordecai raced through the house's front door. Esther had never seen him so stirred up or so out of breathe before.

"Esther come quickly!" Mordecai cried. "The King wants to meet you! He will choose someone to be his queen soon, and he wishes to see you!"

"Really?" Esther asked, with a surprised look on her face.

Esther couldn't believe this was happening. She put on her
fanciest dress and ran outside where Mordecai was waiting.
The two of them started for the palace.

When they reached the palace, they drove up the long and winding driveway. It was larger and fancier than Esther had ever imagined. Esther and Mordecai stepped out of the car and walked arm and arm through the palace's front gate.

They walked past the gardens, around the fountains, through the flowers, and down the l-o-o-o-n-g hall until they reached a giant, golden door.

As Esther reached for the bronze door handle, she paused. She gave cousin Mordecai one last hug and took a deep breath. Then she slowly opened the giant door.

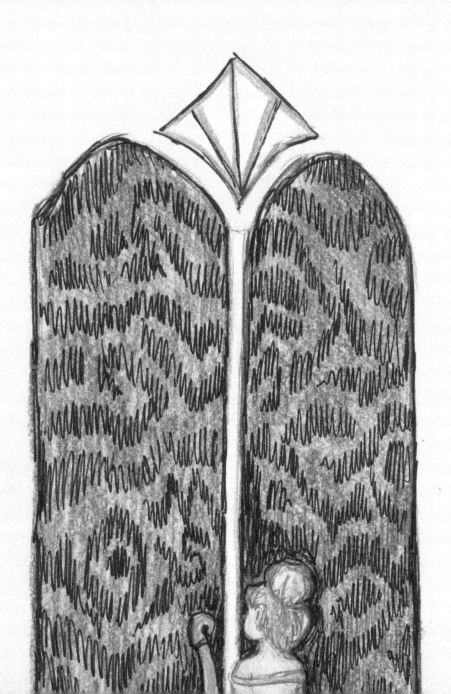

She quietly stepped into a large room filled with gold, silver, and pearls. It was the most beautiful sight Esther had ever seen. She felt like a million tiny butterflies were flying around inside her stomach.

Before she could even open her mouth to introduce herself, the king looked down from his throne. When he saw Esther, his face lit up.

There was something different about her. She seemed so secure, brave, and beautiful. She was different from any other girl the king had ever met. Because of how brave Esther appeared to be, the king knew she was the one he had been searching for.

The King jumped off his throne and asked Esther to be his queen. She couldn't believe it!

Esther smiled her biggest smile. She didn't know how to be a queen or live in a palace but she had a feeling that this was exactly what God wanted her to do.

Later, Esther and the King were married. They had the fanciest, most beautiful wedding Esther could have imagined.

A while after the wedding, on a hot summer day, Mordecai was working at the palace's front gate. He heard two of the guards say mean things about the Jewish people living in the village.

Their friends at the palace didn't know that Esther and Mordecai were Jewish but the guards were talking about everyone Mordecai and Esther loved most. Mordecai felt sad and scared.

Mordecai ran to find Esther and tell her what he had heard. He ran past the fountains, through the flowers, up a twisting, winding staircase until he found Esther.

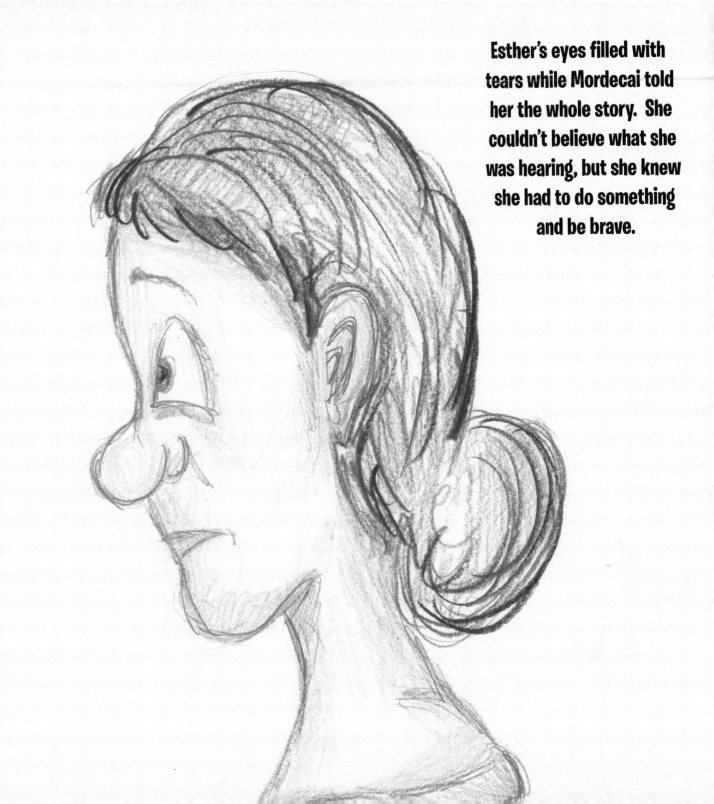

Esther's eyes filled with tears while Mordecai told her the whole story. She couldn't believe what she was hearing, but she knew she had to do something and be brave.

She had to tell the King what Mordecai had heard.
She knew he would know what to do. She ran to the
palace as quickly as her feet could carry her.

She ran past the gardens, around the fountains, through the flowers, down the l-o-o-o-n-g hall until she reached the giant golden door. She opened the big palace door and went inside.

Esther told the King what Mordecai had heard. Her heart broke into a million pieces. She was afraid that someone might try to hurt the Jewish people. She loved these people as much as she loved the king.

The King smiled. He was happy that Esther and Mordecai had the courage to speak up when they knew something was wrong.

That night, the King threw the fanciest party anyone in the village had ever seen. Beautiful cloths covered the tables. Pearls hung from the chandeliers. Vases were filled with flowers.

The light from the many candles made the room glow a pretty yellow. Esther had never seen a room as beautiful as this one.

At the party, Esther sat at a large table and watched everyone have fun. As she watched, Esther knew that God had sent her to the palace for a special reason. God created her to be queen. He did this so that Esther could help save the Jewish people. People who she, Mordecai, and God loved more than anything.

This turned out to be the grand adventure that Esther always wanted.

Printed in the USA
CPSIA information can be obtained
at www.ICGtesting.com
JSHW072027140824
68134JS00043B/3821

9 781683 503163